"Norine Spurling's *poems* reflect a lifetime of attention to experience, to feeling, to thought, which she shapes into words. Her luscious images are color drenched: "milk stained sky", "carmine wash", "bird calls/ a turquoise song", "fading sunset's garnet cast". She uses myth, travel, people to probe for their meanings. Her poems of loss break the heart, though she is unafraid to collect those who passed in the honest assessment of all they meant to her. She surprises the reader with poems that startle and make new. We can understand the "vinegar bones of yesterday" though no one has quite said it like that before. In these poems she carefully elucidates the stages of a woman's life and carefully reflects on all she has known. This beautiful book will call us again and again to enjoy not only the visual imagery but also the sounds of place, time, and memory."

Linda Drajem

Professor of English, SUNY College at Buffalo

Poetry in <u>Poems from the Crooked Circle</u>, 2014, published by Crooked Circle Press

"A richly sensuous diary of the landscapes of love, loss, spirit and inheritance, as transmuted through a painter's mindful eye. Sensitive in all weathers to the pulse and colors of the natural world, Spurling's gently questioning, clear-eyed poems find evocative presences in an ocean that "sighs and weeps / how long, how long"; in tidal ponds, trees, fish, the "squashed red balloon" of a setting sun, a striped blanket, a "rocking canoe" that sits "by my front door". There are many moons here, the bones of ancestors, the mysteries of a half-hidden, melancholy mother and preoccupied father, awakenings and deaths. Now at seventy, with "the harsh truth of the new / already melting into / the sweet myth of the past", she is fully grown, deeply initiated into the "soundless thrumming / of the universe", and ready for anything."

Ann Goldsmith

Author of *The Spaces Between Us*,
published by <u>Outriders Poetry Project</u>,
and *No one Is the Same Again*,
published by <u>The Quarterly Review of Literature</u>
as one of its 1999 prizewinning Poetry Books

Ann's poems have appeared in numerous journals and anthologies.

"This anthology is a travelogue through the verdant forests and cool sweet streams of Norine Spurling's imagination and very real life struggles; an invitation to share and celebrate the quiet, gentle, and contemplative life of one who has been so thoroughly devoted to the arts. It is a reminder, as is the ongoing mission of all poetry, that we need to slow down, to look more closely, to breath more deeply, to hear more intently, to pull our fingers through soil and savor its texture as if born sightless.

"*poems* is clearly to the written word what Norine's paintings and drawings are to the visual arts.

"To those fortunate to have delighted in the latter, this is saying much."

George Grace

Author of *Steeling America*, *Night Wanes*, and *Dawn*

"Having long admired the quiet beauty of Norine Spurling's sensitively wrought drawings and watercolors, I was exceptionally pleased to discover that her widely respected approach to fine art media has found another avenue of expression via the written word. I was stuck by the manner in which she uses color in both disciplines. Her artworks have alternately used either a muted palette or rich jewel tones and her poems are also liberally infused with metaphorically rich references to color. In both cases, it is the color – both visual and verbal – that effectively stimulates the imagination of the viewer/reader. Norine's poems are evocative musings on the often "unregarded moments" of nature and personal relationships. Her dexterous manipulation of language puts those distinct places, times and experiences into focus with precision and clarity. Through her poetry, she powerfully conveys her heightened perception – an astute view of an artist - of the natural world."

Gerald Mead

Independent curator, art collector and arts writer, who teaches in the Design Department at SUNY College at Buffalo

poems

Poem

I want to write a poem
That will lay on the page
In fluid snake-like form
Winding along the river
From stone to stone
Carrying its message
In small fairy boats
Blue skies and cloud castles
Reflecting in its surface
Liquid silver fishes
Lost in its shadows
A poem of mystery and revelation
A parallel world

poems

by
Norine Spurling

Buffalo Arts Publishing
Tonawanda, New York

Copyright © 2014
Norine Spurling

All rights reserved,
including the right of reproduction
in whole or in part in any form.

Cover image from a collage by Russell Ram

Buffalo Arts Publishing
Tonawanda, New York

ISBN 978-0615931791
Printed in the USA

Dedicated to the memory of my lost loves and those who wait for me beneath the sunlit stones.

Thanks to the Women of the Crooked Circle whose friendship and encouragement helped me through a time of loss and recovery and who helped me to right my little canoe.

This book could not have come together without the enormous patience and guidance of my dear friend Jimmie Gilliam.

Thanks to my dear friend Russell Ram for his collage which we used on the cover and which so clearly echoes the feeling of my poems.

Contents

MILLENNIUM 11

HEARTWORDS 25

LOST LOVES 43

MOTHER 59

ANCESTORS 67

SILENCE 85

PEOPLE 95

PLACES 127

SEASONS 141

ENDINGS 169

About the Author 178

The River

The river is dark
wider than the sky
waiting there
on a wing of silence
half cold
yet quietly – new

MILLENNIUM

Opening

The eye of the sleeping morning
rises soft as blue silk
rolling out of the velvet darkness
streaking the horizon
in narrow wooly bands
of peach and pearl
slowly lifting the great eyelid
of the heaven
stirring the heartbeat beneath
as the Earth awakes
to sing her morning song
and the sun rising
leaves drops of pure gold
to emboss the top of each wave
and the shore
rough as a kitten's tongue
receives the creamy foam
at the edge of the day

Threshold

The sun hovers
a squashed red balloon
on the horizon
an aquanaut
in blazing helmet
poised to dive into
oblivion
set to make his
mighty circuit
down the watery
corridors of night
dragging his star spangled
coverlet behind him

On the edge of another day
another continent
he rises ashen
through a silver mist
leaves his brother stars behind
while alone he braves
the pale blue heaven
an astronaut
in Orion's stolen armor
fireproof he regains
his throne once more

A Canoe Among the Columns

Imagine with me a hillside, green, wet,
with misty rain and ancient stones
the shriek of birds
sweeping the opal sky
cadence of sneakers
on the wooden slatted path
or on the sucking grass
who wouldn't want to hide here
huddled in this magic space
feel the pulse, the heavy breath,
the creak of sweaty sinews
visioned ancients
laboring on the moor
to carry this crude gift
this almighty ring
this wordless prayer
to this holy place
hide here with me
in my secret cave
wrap in my hoary blanket
lean against the damp oars
around us the waves
of the old millennium
still rake the fires of the universe

Ace (Icarus)

Walls surround
dark fragments
of weeping rock
dank and slime
a lid-less tomb

standing here
this foolhardy son
of ancient Greece
thinks he is a flying machine
his arms outstretched
stitched with feathers
pale and strong
he aims to soar above this place
to wander among the floating
lambs of Zeus
so pale they are
against the azure dome
and thus he rises

on glistening wings
high into the sunlit silence
looking down
he sees the ocean
aqua pale and flat
surrounds a little
patch of green
too small to house
a Minoan king

poems

he feels a sudden wind
a flame, an ending in
the nether world

for down he goes
to meet the sea
that rises up to greet him
to gather up the broken wing
and scattered feathers
the wreckage
of his heroic
flying machine

Night On Water

Last night I slept
in my canoe
the sky above
an upturned enamel bowl
star spattered
and rimmed in the bloody
memory of the dying sun
below me the shallow water
sucked at the stones
along the shore
and shot fiery lights
to the stars overhead
in the east a wonderful moon
came sliding up
from the ocean's edge
all opaline and crackling
in the night's salt air
wrapped in its own
diaphanous cloak
a cottony wisp of cloud
a sigh
that rocked my boat
my pale cocoon
with gentian stripe

Dust Motes

In the gloaming
of the forest glen
stands an abandoned
cottage where
teacups rattle darkly
behind glass doors
teacups stained
sienna red touched
with hemlock gray
and flecked yet
with small black shards
unread predictions
scattered black dots
like constellations
driven from the sky
burned spacecraft
with no dreams
to share
the musty smell
of faded green linoleum
rises up
like dust motes
in the watered sun
alien life rafts
aching to go home
to reawaken
those blackened leaves
and recover from them
the dreams left lying there
in that moldering heartplace

The Temple Tiger

The tongue of the temple bell
tolls over the velvet hills
piercing the purple eye
of the striped tiger that paces
in the splintered sun

The sun's splintered rays
rebound against the temple walls
and echo past the velvet hill
where the striped tiger sits
amid the purple shadows

The purple evening hour
drapes the sky and
cloaks the temple wall
in velvet shadow as the
splintered tiger paces on

The tiger paces past the temple
on patient purple paws
his golden eyes reflect
the splintered sun
that invades his velvet path

His velvet coat ripples
into splintering stripes
among the purple shadows
and the tiger nears
the temple steps

The temple splinters into
purple vapor before
the tiger's velvet paws

HEARTWORDS

My Canoe

A canoe sits by my front door
it floats there on the grass and dry leaves
it bobs up and down in the moonlight
pale and curved like the moon itself
there is a red star painted on its bow
crisp edged as a bread knife
red as the sunset sky at evening
in the morning I shall put on my moccasins
and sail away to where the West begins
to the place where the land
rises up blue as broken glass
and the lakes are deeper than any ocean
and I shall lie there
on my striped woolen blanket
under a dome of stars
beside my rocking canoe
but first I must do the laundry
and rake the yellow leaves
for as sure as Monday follows Sunday
and day follows night
my canoe may leave without me

Night by the Sea

Branches creak
black shadows strike
against a milk stained sky

the ocean sighs and weeps
how long, how long

a hammock creaks
seabird calls
moonlight drips
through a crack
in the wall
shadows of cedar
bleed across the floor

small boat dips
by the rocks at the shore
tugs to be free
of its tethered cord

how long, how long

Rainbows

The house stands lonely
by the wet sand
the sea as hard as steel
the wind skips by

the wind slips by
the open door
the woman holds a silver cup
an autumn rose

and in her ample hand
a turquoise bowl
beside the door
a yellow broom

her hand is brown
the sky is blue
her socks are low
the rug itself is red

she pauses now within
an amber haze
the early morning
scent of baking bread

I have not often seen
rainbows such as this

Summer Evening at the Lake

The setting sun
draws a carmine wash
across the sky
ripples its red wake
through the deep blue
face of the lake
stars begin to press
against the heavens
fog gently rising
trees fade to gray ghosts
behind a row of little summer cabins
pale faces pierced
with golden supper-lit windows
fireflies weave heavily
among the grasses
stirring memories
of children's laughter
on the chill evening air
as the day folds into
the coverlet of night

Totem Secrets

Three canoes shiver to rest
on the pebbled island shore
dark pines crowd the sandy edge

nine women move into
the forest's shadowed nest
where circled tents await

strangers meeting in
the fading light
unfamiliar voices newly met

whisper secrets hesitant as
the darkness that surrounds
totem truths half surrendered

small creatures rustle
in the dry grass
a bird calls and is quiet

somewhere a lonely sigh

three canoes wait
in the faint moonlight

Heartwords

Words that speak
with the aquamarine clarity
of the effervescent ocean
sit like salt upon the tongue
set the heart to hemorrhaging
that echo across the universe
with rhythms that beat
upon the sandy shore
and set the rocks to ringing
rejoicing with the gulls
that soar in the crystal air of winter
resounding in the bell of sky

Treetops

At night the treetops
lie against the western sky
hunching there
like Monet's haystacks
softly rounded
in their constancy
they stand between me
and the pallid void of night
comforting my dreams
commanding sleep
wrapping me
in Monet's mists
and remembered rainbow hues

Night Rain

The rain comes like
a train in the night
grumbling and rumbling
its way through my neighborhood
I lay there wakeful
pondering the paintings
on the bedroom wall
emerald green leaves
spread serenely from pots
seashells – a Japanese plate
a seahorse
sleeping in a sea blue room
quiet except for the
insistent thought images
that pass across
the interior of my eyes
a silent movie
sans popcorn, flickering lights
rustle of candy wrappers
in the dark
no dramatic swelling music
foretelling danger to the heroine
or a romantic interlude
all this overshadowed now
by the soporific hum
in my tinnitic inner ear
and the surging sound
of falling rain

They Say

They say that
skies are bluer
clouds are whiter
    in foreign lands

moon is clearer
sun is brighter
    in our infant past

but I say
days are longer
sleep is deeper
    in this new place

my old quilt
has been replaced
by cool blue sheets
my pillow nestles
in the evening light
in the shock of change
an earthquake in my soul
has shaken out
the old forgetfulness
and unfurled
the vibrant flag of life

Death Song

Three loveliest things
moonlight on my pillow
oranges in a blue bowl
the imprint of your hand in mine
but soon I go to seek the sunset

LOST LOVES

Strange

Strange how my heart breaks
on this foreign shore
hollyhock and tea rose
still climb by the door
blue sky and sunshine
sharp enough to cut my flesh

Strange how my heart aches
to be here once again
alone among the blossoms
and the summer bees
once I cut you from my life
pruning back dead trees

I thought you'd gone for good
along with summer days
and camping in the wood
strange how you linger here
to break my heart again

Dear Lost One

Dear lost one
the bird that fled my life
    I recall the day I gave you back
    to your sweet mother
    enclosed in a golden urn
    and laid you under a flat white stone
would you have found her
had I not laid you by her feet
    I felt you fly to her breast
    did you pause on your way
    to remember me
how could you when I had turned
without a thought for you
throwing off my widow's veil
under the hallowed sun
stepping so eagerly into
the onrushing gale
    it is time now for me
    to remember you
    to cast off the veil of resentment
    that blinds my eye
    that binds my heart
begin to search
the detritus of our past
for those few shining particles
of genuine gold
time before I too must take flight
    who will welcome me
    will you be there
    or have I turned too many
    of life's pages into
    unredeemable ash

Loss

It was March when you left me
melted snow dripping from eaves
icy tears washing my face

Your old chair still warm
your coffee cup half full
your tattered robe still on the hook
your weary slippers by the door

Your bed, not shared for months
seemed cold and dry
wan as the wintery sun
that glazed the window pane

I could not forgive you
for going then
nor could I had you stayed

There was a June once
full of promise it was
flowers filled the rooms
and church bells
summer days of laughter
autumns crisp and golden
winters filled with pine scent
and red ribbon bows

But they left before you did my love
so take your rest
wherever you may be
and should forgiveness come
let it

You Went Away

Suddenly you went away
drew a breath and left
I think I am going now
you'd said. I thought
no, not such as you
belligerent and brave
so cock-sure and yet,
you did bluff and bluster some
but you trusted their magic
how were you to know
how little magic was left

Ours was no great romance
yet there were times
when the chasm between
our two selves seemed to shrink
and we drifted closer
like two barges
drawn by the river's current
a rough facsimile of love

Tall He Was

Tall as a giraffe he was
and dry as a post
hands that fluttered and flew
like hawks in the wind
crows in the road
his voice like sand
on a wooden floor
winter wind on a
desert afternoon
yet when he cast his eyes at me
the desert bloomed
purple and magenta
like the pulse in my throat
an ocean's salt roar
a sheer rock fall

Lost

I am
the lost daughter
walking by the sea
over bruised rocks
vinegar bones of yesterday
this is the river I knew you by
this pounding bit of sea
this ocean devoid of praise
storm clouds lurking
behind the cypress tree
you the man from nothing
once a necessary light
field guide to heaven
slippery rock by the sea

Rag Doll

Raggedy little doll
my name across your chest
I can't remember hugging you
or if I loved you best

It was dear old Auntie's hands
that fashioned you this way
that capped your hair in yellow
that sewed your pale blue eye

A little flapper girl you are
belted at the hip
with dashing pink edged scarf
wrapped around your neck

What was it that we called you
tucked by me in my bed
was it Polly or was it Sally
I know it wasn't Ned

Yellow-stained I take you now
from your cedar chest
I kept you all these years
I must have loved you best

Persephone

My mother had a storage chest
as large as a coffin
with a lid as heavy
as that ancient one in Palestine
I often begged to see
what nestled there among
the spicy smells of cedar wood
the warmer memories of wool
of winter nights with firelight
that flickered across the oaken floor
once I lifted up the lid
and there within that scented tomb
lay this little pallid doll
her cotton body pale as death
eyes of watercolor blue
bobbed hair described in yellow yarn
my name embroidered on her breast
and like Persephone
she calls me back
to my old nursery again
the aroma of warm sweet milk
surrounds me
laundry soap and sun
my mother's breath
and this old doll, much younger then
abandoned among
the bedclothes of my memory

MOTHER

She Died

She died
she just closed her eyes and left
left without saying goodbye
we laid her before the altar
in a casket piled with flowers
a summer garden
of pinks and forget-me-nots
we saw her there
hands folded on her blue dress
her face pale
her tightly curled
brown lashes stitching
her blue eyes closed
and we did not recognize her
as she lay there before
the old altar in the old church
the place where we sang
Christmas carols
candles in the windows
stars in the deep vault
of the sky above
we carried her to her grave
her white-washed house
on the side of the hill
a house where others wait
in silent stillness

poems

in musty darkness
a white-washed home for the dead
among ferns and wild roses
facing the eastern sun
looking toward Jerusalem

She died, this woman
with the blue-gray eyes
grayer than the blue of summer
bluer than the clouds of winter
clear as water in a silver bowl
but once she lived
read fairy tales to her babies
on a red plaid blanket
under the cedar trees
or picnicked
on the grassy hill
among prickly pears
and purple fruited cactuses
where cries of white sea birds
echo on the air
and down the rocky shore
she would never dare to fling herself
into the ocean's ultramarine depths
but gathered
purple periwinkles
and bits of ruby crab shells
cast-off detritus
from the lace-edged turquoise sea
the sky-blue sea
the sometimes gray-blue sea
that stretches smooth
as far as Africa
that in winter heaves

its dark surface at the clouds
or crashes green against the rocks
and in summer reaches sunward
before rolling into
salty indigo valleys
as her babies grew foreign
in their busy lives
her sadness drew her in
like a crab into its rocky den
fearful to move out onto the flat sand
watching life through
a murky window
thickened green
as sand-washed glass
and so she died
she didn't wait to say goodbye
she gathered up her memories
like jewels from the sea
salty and sandy and
filled with cast-off bits
of other lives
she closed her blue-gray eyes
her gray-blue eyes
the color of the quiet ocean
and with a sigh
turned her face
toward Jerusalem

Mother

Mother you told of flying home
freshly released from
files and steno pad
hair damp flush faced
rushing
to kitchen table wicker chair
patchwork coverlet
dark haired love

Can this have been you
this calm closed face I last saw
at rest among the
fragrant blossoms
wordless unforgiving

In the churchyard now
I walk the mossy stones
lay my hand on
the sun-warmed deck
the whited slab of your dark cave
and I see you there
pale shadow among the palm trees
or sitting like stone by the shore

And I cry out
what did I do to lose you
how was it that I hurt you
with my anxious need to be
alone in this god-forsaken world
can I come to you again
as I did as a child

poems

I cry out in silence
will you welcome me
when my time is done
my bones and ashes
warm from the annealing oven
will you let me join you
in your stone-walled cavern
among the sweet blue flowers
and the yellow bees
will you tell me that you love me

The Little Book

I knew you as my mother
a warm stranger in periwinkle blue
already fading from the ruby hearted
truth you once knew
as a tender petal
with a golden dream
you penned your name
in the back of this little book
and filled it with the names
of those you loved
and the ones who lived
on the branches of
your family tree
then he came along
to woo you with his
dark and handsome self
the Adonis of
those golden dreams
you put on white lace
and danced beside the
rushing falls
sang out to the soaring spray
the shouting birds
the little boat
that glides among the rapids
you saw your life arc forward
like the rainbow shining there
but somehow it faded
as the years tumbled on
like the rocks along the shore

poems

and now I look at
this little book
your name inscribed
in the back
so dear and hopeful then
struck through with
masculine assurance and
replaced by his
strong hand

ANCESTORS

Upstate Farm House

This was a farm once
this green slice of land

the pig pen there
now overflows
with bachelor buttons
purple hyacinth and weeds

weeds that grow and thrive
like the rangy brown boys
who used to live here

boys whose voices echo yet
among the maple trees
and grasses

voices now grown hushed
as the breeze that races
round the barn
on this late September day

Stones

They stand in stolid rows
up and down the hill
square stones the color
of warm bones
      cool pearls
           smooth eggs
engraved with names
      from the past
           they live yet
for those who remember
those who come quiet
in the afternoon
lace handkerchiefed
in the fading sun
to lay a yellow rose
      a purple ribbon
           a spangled flag
at the feet of these very stones
these aged rocks
      these monuments to love
mouldering beneath these ferns
      beside this path
in the convex mirror of the mind
      they stand there
           side by side
Nina and her man James Moore
their hands farm-stained
      work hardened
           gently loved
and they gaze   beyond the hill
to the old farmhouse
where their children
struggled to be born
to take their first hard gasp of life

Song in a Cemetery

I have come here calling
with Nina's grandson John
he with cane and crippled foot
and great granddaughter Jane
she with Nina's curls
and computer filled with forebears
we come searching now for Nina
and her man James Moore

We walk the winding path
between the stolid stones
looking for a name
that will reckon up the past
and here they stand
the ones we seek
Nina boldly upright
next to her man James Moore

No moss has crept upon them
to eat away their names
they stand alone
their children gone
to grace some other hillside
but now, who else remembers Nina
and her man James Moore

Who has left these yellow flowers
beside these weathered stones

Autumn Rose

Late the tall grass bowed
to the mower's blade
its buzzing hum quieting the bees
leaving a quilt of silence
in its fragrant wake
and as the day begins to fade
the autumn rose may bow its head
its petals falling
pallid petroglyphs of a summer gone
pale fragments in the dying sun
drifting in the graying light
among the graven stones
remembrance of
old lost loves
mother, father, aunt Marie
the Wilsons all in formal row
underneath the golden oak
while cars pass homeward bound
other thoughts concern
now the azure night descends
bathing the sweet petals
in purple shadow

Where He Lies

The stone beneath which
My grandfather's
First love lies
Is blinding in the
Springtime sun
His name is etched
Beside her own
But I ask not
Where his bones lie

The Old Photograph

The distance lies between them
An uneven white sheet
Startling as a
Summer's wash line
Solid as a whitewashed wall
Pressing them against
The side frames of the
Anxious photograph
The document
Of their wedded life

Big Boys Don't Cry

The boys are waiting
by the cemetery gate
their white shirts smell
of laundry soap
and summer hedges
their pants of cedar chest
and winter nights
their heads are warm
from mother's hand
damp and yeasty
on each smooth brow
salty now
as fresh churned butter

The boys stand still
in the noon day sun
kites and string at hand
but daddy's gone
he's lying now
beneath a new white stone

Morning

The sun comes in
through the half-drawn shade
a small puddle
on the worn linoleum

The trees outside
fill it with color
the waking birds
fill it with sound

Slowly it steals across the room
silently it scales the wall
finds the coffee cup
the old blue bowl

I reach for the shade
and the sun slams in
to break the trembling dawn
into fiery day

Treachery

Silver the light
sparkles it across
the kitchen floor
where once
slipped I
bone-cracked
and groaning
pain blue
and lavender
tears stream
the floor
polished now
new bone-breaks
inviting

Today

the day is heavy
dark   wet
sunflowers peer
at the sodden ground
no sun today
no cicada's staccato song

SILENCE

Defiance

I give you my anger
Silent as stone
Icy as mountain pass
Orbs of rock here
Dark crystals on this venomous plate
Leaking light
From ancient saline depths
Chilled by polar currents
Oozing silent secrets
Dug from elder times
Unknowable
Unspeakable
Tongueless
Eyeless
Breathing words
I cannot speak
Cracking like ice
Before your Saharan eyes

Here and There

You are there
I am here
You were here
You were always here
Now you have gone
And left me here
I was not always here
You brought me here
Here where you were
Where you had always been
I was glad to be here
To be with you in this place
I liked it here
It reminded me of where I used to be
Now it reminds me of you
And I wonder if
You like it there
Where you have gone
Or would you rather be here
Here in this place
Now that I am here alone
Or are you happy there
As I am
Here without you

Swept Away

She pedaled through emerald boughs
laced with saffron in the sun
kicked up her heels in garnet shoes
bronze legs spinning
her laughter hit him in his groin
her hazel eyes slashed against
his golden skin
his ribs unfurled
she swung him out against the universe
ripped out his heart
and dashed it on the rocks
he felt the salt waves rush
about him and
fill his ears with sand
he rose up like a giant seabird
caught her ruby wings in his
stopped her breath with his breath
blotted out the sun
and changed her name to his

Fragment

When spring comes
all pink and white
and the sky's a misty blue
I hear the pines whisper on the hill
echoes of a summer chant
a sickle moon above the meadows
damp salt breezes
rustling in the sawgrass
and you young and brown again
and in my heart
fragments of a forgotten song

Silence at 2am

There is a silence at 2am
that catches in the throat
washes color from the open eye
crowds the straining ear with sigh
and fills the room with creaking weight

There is a lightness to the body
lifted by the surge of wakefulness
the soundless thrumming
of the universe
the creaking swell of silence

Then there is an openness
for a weary mind
to bid its fears to fade away
and sleep return its blessedness
in quiet dream
that stills the restless silence once again

PEOPLE

Vermeer

The artist sits in his studio
shirt black-striped
stockings red
his brush against the canvas

on the far wall a map
of the old world
golden faded emblem
of a wider dream

in the slanting rays of the sun
a young muse in blue
her violin echoing
an amber chord
against the silence

he leans forward
black stripes straining
feet planted on the
checkered floor
bright scarlet hose

she turns toward him
caught now in the silvering light
blue feathers in her hair
violin asleep in her hand
sealed against time
his silent symphony

Untitled

Each day she emerges
into the warm light of morning
to the blue sky
the trees   the paved street
the face beneath the helmet
the child's fragile playful smile
the actress   the clown
the old woman   the young man
she captures all in her loving eye
her one cyclopean eye
the play of light and shadow
on the brick wall
the way a face is lit
against a dark drape
a figure by a window
the music of the day
these she carries back
to her dark cave
where she fixes them with magic
to white edged pages
and like dry October leaves
they retain the bitter sweet
aroma of our lives

Talking to Helen (Keller)

What a miracle is speech
how strange the words
how deep
how sharp the knife
how keen the pain
how cold the water
clear and cold
it pours like silk
runs across the fingers
blue as ice
shaping letters on the palm
upon the tongue
a breath
a summer breeze
a memory
in shades and shadows
purple as the folding hills
golden as the tall grass
a whispered blessing
a gentle touch
an apocalyptic stroke

Oh Sally

She is sitting in her garage
in her white plastic chair
knuckled fingers braided
in the hammock of her lap
house dress stretched
across splayed knees
two hillocks and a valley
sprinkled in faded spring blossoms
her hair a pale gray mist
eyes lost behind thick glasses
feet wrapped in blue felt slippers

How long has she been sitting there
does she know   does she care
has her mind become as clean and pure
as her white plastic chair
do we hear her cry out
in the darkness of the night
Oh Sally you mean thing
and does she look for her
among the undies in her drawer
or beneath her purple cotton dress
its passions long spent

Was Sally her little sister
the one who stole her beau
who later found a big fat toad
among the undies in her drawer
and did Mama make her sit like this
in a hard white kitchen chair
her supple pink fingers braided
in the hammock of her dress
tear drops blending into
the purple blossoms of its hem

Sunset

All day she holds herself
pale skin peeling
      like onion
           like aspen
revealing blue veins
      plum bruises
her spine a chain
square-cut ivory
held straight
in fear of bending
toward the cane
      the walker
the flowered cotton dress
she sings her song
and writes her life
upon her parchment skin
in runic verse
across her cheek
      her wrist
           her knee
and hangs her dreams
like rags upon a tree
old ghosts upon the hill
where someone waits

She Wore a Blue Veil

She wore a blue veil and down-cast eyes
she carried a crook and searched the meadow
she did as she pleased – the world be damned

she was touched by a feathered breath and sighed
she longed for a warm woolen coat and wept
she put a red poppy in her hat and laughed

she was told she was blessed
she was told she was lost
she was told she was contrary

the world called her mother
they sang songs about her
they found her odd but lovable

they called her Mary

Night Managers

The night managers of life
are ordinary women
owners of the cooling palm
the calming word
they stable the steeds of darkness
reign in the prancing fears
the flashing hooves of panic
taking the last watch
as the sun again rises
they celebrate the earth
and sweep away the dust
left by the pale horses of night

Passing

Under a brilliant sun
they move
away from each other
as if parting forever
yet only a moment
are they caught here
frozen
in the searing heat of the sun
the fading passion of a smile
the harsh truth of the new
already melting into
the sweet myth of the past
they glance
down the long green slope
toward the constant ocean
tumbling headlong into
the ragged future

and the yellow buttercups
keep their silence

Mary

A flutter of wings by the window
with a start she turns
toward the light
the shaft of light
that strikes the sill
to fall in a puddle
on the oaken floor

She wraps her blue scarf
over her tawny hair
hides her brow, her breast,
her bones, her lungs, her legs
I am not the one you want
she cries, I'm a good girl
I don't do that

The Girl in the Blue Plaid Skirt

The girl in the blue plaid skirt
has measured the statue's head
has drawn it carefully in chalk

now, she smokes a cigarette
she feels like Lana Turner
sitting on the steps by
the fountain at 20th and Race
her hair is brown
it lays on her cheek
like a robin's wing

the girl in the blue plaid skirt
sits in the fading light
Lana Turner on a park bench

Fatherhood

Father, that old gypsy
misty brown as a November
morning early on the meadow
a leather trickster in the woods
carving figures with his pocket knife
flashy handkerchief around his head
his children soon forgotten
as the wood chips 'round his feet
a kiss, a tousled head
and off he goes again
to some mysterious occupation
beyond our infant ken
so tall and strong and clever
oh to know the mystery of his world
to go with him on his shoulder
to be allowed a pocket knife

Flight of Foolish Fancy

Yon fair maiden's fiddle
is full of fingerprints
foul, filmy fingerprints
some fresh, some forgotten
many forged in feeling
at four am on Friday last
here at the edge of the field
by the fence where the ferns grow
a stream runs
between the fir trees
that stand like a fortress
our fair maiden
runs at a feverish pace
footprints dent the sand
beside the frothy stream
where fish swim to and fro
and a feather from yon flying bird
floats gently upon the flowing water
I fear our faithless maiden
has forgotten to fetch
the fake fur that was furnished to her
by her former friend
the fusty fortune teller
who will surely fuss and fume
if she finds out
but right now she fantasizes
about the handsome fiddle player
with the freckled flanks
who made such fabulous music
with his fingers upon her fiddle
last Friday night

Lambanema

The ancestors' bones
are joyful tonight
the sun sets
the stars crackle
in the dome of night
shining faces circle
teeth aglitter
spilling out
the old songs
in the smoke filled air
eyes grow large
at the awful tales
great grandfather's
battles of the long ago

perhaps the old bones
will dance with us tonight

Fairy Tales for Gremlin Babies

I shall walk across the flat ocean
leave no footprints
on its gleaming surface
I will go to the other side
where you can no longer see me
and I will hide there
among the bright umbrella trees
where rain falls like diamonds
sliding down a silken rainbow
tumbling into an azure sky
a sky that at night is stitched
with stars and silver hairpins
and I shall bring you
baskets filled with plantains
yams and golden mangoes
to feed your hungry souls
panting like goldfish
at the edge of the pool

Selena

In the first chill of October
you follow me all the way home
your amber golden face
      somewhat askew
as you always are mid-month
and   as I pull into my driveway
you hide behind the maple tree
paler now   a shy specter
      caught in its branches
when I go to my bed
          you are still there
peeking timidly
      through the blind
just as you did
      that first fall night
         a million years ago

I love you now   as I did then
      Luna, Diana, Selena
         Princess of the sky

Old Friend

Dear old friend
where have you gone
how far from here to there
are you happy where you are
do you ever think of me
is your life as rich
as red wine
as sweet as cotton candy

Can I join you when
I am old and gray
and life has lost its zest
will you meet me at the gate
with St. Peter and the rest

PLACES

Belize

It was Sunday   in Belize
the sandy road
snakes between
jungle walls
dust rises round our feet
like spray around
the bow of an ocean liner
somewhere a bird calls
a turquoise song
filled with sun
the heat of noon and
up ahead the ancient ruins
gray stones piled jagged
patterned paths
edging the broad green field
where deadly games
once played and
men wore blood red feathers
on their heads
I hear them shouting
chanting in an arcane tongue
and you are standing there
close enough to touch
your eyes brown pools
swarthy hands at rest but
you were not there
that Sunday   in Belize

Machu Picchu

Heart-pounding, breathless
I climb the ragged trail
along the
cloud snagged mountains
standing dark
against the morning sky
below me now
laced in mist
ancient Machu Picchu
rests among the peaks
a curving plain
of massive stones
marble white
shimmering
within the green tiered slopes
this jewel
chalice of stone and rock
atop the Andes

overhead
a careless condor floats
on the restless air

Mustard Flowers

My maple tree is yellow now
yellow as the mustard flowers
I remember growing along
the dusty road
in a land by the azure sea
and those warm afternoons
when we brought home
salty fists full
of drooping mustard flowers
gifts for our canary Fred
his body pulsing
soft as his song
feet as sharp as
mustard against the tongue
he sits muttering in his cage
by the shadowed dining table
or singing his golden notes
against the sky-blue
window pane
his yellow body a reflection
in the watery pool of
the polished table top

Skinny Dipping

The moon hangs over us
a Chinese lantern in the summer sky
its reflection skates
toward the rocky shore
skipping over the ripples
of the water's surface

Beneath us our legs are
pale extensions
of the moon's liquid self
moving like seaweeds in the current
slowly we move our hands
in broad circles
making starry traces
through the dark sea
as our toes reach down
into the soundless depths
where the noonday fishes sleep

Now moving together
through the soft warm air
we touch cool lips
to chill cheeks
then slip under the surface
sliding along a wavering
moonray to test the depth

The Fish Pond

I lean on the smooth rail
The curve of a Japanese bridge
My reflection crisp on the water
Your dark shadow rippling behind me
I was as young as the bright fish below us
You had blue eyes
and thought you knew it all
When the rain fell
It shattered everything

In the Gift Shop

A wild man looks down from the wall
pink faced timekeeper of the universe
sailor from an ancient magic ship
counting out the hours
        somewhere someone
strokes a finger harp
a note that startles
in its crystal clarity
fading gently into dusk
        footsteps pass on the street
a laugh, a word,
and silence once again
among the hues of autumn
the golden leaf that curls
the fading sunset's garnet cast
        the mirror on the wall
a smooth reflecting pool
passage into wonder
anchorage for a magic ship
        where does the wild man go
when the light is gone?

Under the Trees

The moon has risen silver
the lake a lamé tablecloth
lying wrinkled
in the fold of the hill
and just there
on the right
that woman under the trees
her dress turning shades of lavender
hairpins falling from her braids
like small stars
on their pilgrimage
in August
what is she doing
under the trees?

Tall grasses curl about my feet
cool and wet and
deeply green
as I step away among
the shadows down the hill
and creep slowly
toward the lake – the trees
the moon – the falling stars
where has she gone
that woman under the trees
that shadow with flowing hair

Winter

Today my backyard
is snow-swallowed
fall flowers   winter dead
brush marks on a white page
a tranquil haiku verse

SEASONS

In Buffalo

Spring is

Hard arriving

We search for

The hiding sun

Shiver in

Winter coats

As leaves burst

Grass greens

Tulips push

The earth cracks

The axis tilts

And we are thrust

Suddenly

Into summer's

Oven blast

Black Eyes

Black-eyed susans hunker drunkenly
Under the evergreen hedge

They nod to each other knowingly
As the wind sighs overhead

The cat peeks at them warily
From behind the picket fence

The old black crow shifts wearily
And screams from the top of the house

August

The towels hang
white and stiff
in the hard sun
where the bees
wobble breathless
and the sultry air
sits on my shoulder
with the weight of that
brown velvet cape
you used to wear
when the snow fell
sharp and light
and the hard sun
cracked like glass

Tidal Pond at Noon

High sun
ripples where
oily rainbows dance
across the fragile blue
fresco of its face
pale clouds stray there
shadows diving
into the caves of its depths
where a lone yellow fish
finds its way
between curtains
of brown seaweed
searching
shells and stones
mute golden queen
of this sunless domain

poems

Summer

Today my office window
is three quarters filled with sky
the top of a green maple
flung against its shallow blueness
in a pattern of fingerling leaves
and fractured light
and through its angled eye
dust motes dance along a sunbeam
into my ordered day
inviting walks and other
careless doings
along a tipsy sidewalk
by the summer road
that leads to nearby
cow kissed hills
and fields of blue-eyed daisies

Haaaah!

Behold

A field of happy sunflowers
much noise among the bees
creatures skitter in the shadows
the flowers stand tall
reach to see the sun
the blue sky
strain against each other
laughing together
pushing and shoving joyously
a sunflower party!

As the sun sets
they bow their heads
sighing in the cool night air
all is quiet in the field
the bees have gone to bed
honey-filled
the field mouse
tweaks his whiskers silently

haaaah!

shhhhh!

More Rain

The sky a graphite blue
           charcoal pewter lead

willow tree weeping
           absinthe mustard callow

along the curve a maple tree
           naked barren stripped

wind and rain stinging
           orange copper spice

           – not a duck around

September

Can this be September
the sun still strikes
his anvil in the lowering sky
still drapes a shadow
across the grass
long and sweet
as any summer day
the bees are working
in the garden yet
and children peddle by
on tinkling bikes
at home their mothers
count the days
the pens, the notebooks
ruled in tidy stripes of blue
lay out the sneakers not yet worn
the t-shirts and the denim jeans
oh September is a cruel month
it fools us with its sunny warmth
while all the time it marches on
toward the frigid days of winter

Autumn

Yellow mums spatter the garden
gentle Monet spots of color
stars in a sea of green
they dance in the late-day breeze
nodding toward the northern sky
quivering at the scent of autumn
that giddy emissary of brooding winter
who comes now in her red-gold gown
trailing over the rusty hills
the ragged fields of corn
whispers to the trees
and spreads her golden cape
across the lawn

By My Back Door

By my back door
a mound of snow has gathered
crept there in the night
and in the long windy days
gloomy as a ghost
in the unlit hour of evening
translucent in reflection
from my kitchen window

It seemed just yesterday
the sun was shining there
yellow daisies nodding
beside the old red barn
birds flying against the sky
and my old canoe
white as the frozen coverlet
now spreading over it all

Winter Afternoon

The maple tree
weaves its golden branches
behind the yellow slats
of my window blind
gold threads
in the late day sun
a tapestry
woven against
the pale blue sky

Song

My song is a dirge
for the falling leaves
now that October
has cast her golden glow
against the darkening sky
and Autumn has thrown
her patchwork quilt
across the sleepy hills
where Winter hides
his icy breath

poems

The Year of the Crocodile

It is the year of the crocodile
when the hen grows fat
and the moon smiles
on the dark ocean
like the mad fisherman
who flings his line
by the sea wall
his boat tied securely
against the stairs
that lead into
the blackening water
and the swimming fishes
lift eye and nose
toward the starry sky

trusting in someone
trusting in no one

Evensong

An egret stands
on the sighing shore

sun over the marshes
      a bloody heart of flame

overhead
      a ragged train of geese
      slashes the graying sky

the rower pauses in his stroke
      boat sliding forward
      on the satin surface

his reflection
      riding silently
      upside down
      below him

and all around
a whisper of eternity
      as the world fades into
      pearlescent dream

Dreams

Dreams may die and slip away
in the dreary days of winter
my old hopes seem lost
beneath the frozen snow
but wait a yellow crocus
sleeps there

ENDINGS

February

Now is the time of ash and bone
days when old snow
lies by the roadside
the ashes of winter
bare bones of an old year
gone weary and dry
waiting breathless
and gray of face
for birthing sounds
to stir beneath
the blue-gray feet of sky
buried in the muddy arc of earth
where hollow bones reverberate
in silent prayer
a new world whispers
against the echoing clime
edges slowly toward
that hosannah morning
that lies beyond the wooded hill

At Seventy

I have brought my life as far as this
now broad-sailed in the golden fullness
of summer
to the secret element of water
where the thread of ripeness
turns away from
the fragile veins of winter
the melancholy melon-colored sun
grows larger on the rim of the sea
sustained by the infinite
and my craft sails on
keel cutting into an even darker blue
bow straining toward
the chorus of the sun's salty setting

This Moment

This moment of dying
the end to which our lives
insistently move
rolling us toward
the ashes, the smoke
the fires of home
the welcoming arms
of remembered loves
a misty relief
from the agony of living
dark corridors
that we cannot understand
any more than we can
remember the
bloody corridors of birth
the cries that surely
follow our leaving
are as lost to our senses
as those that precede
our arrival into this life
this murky ocean
where we reach out
on our loneliness
to touch each other
as with gloved hands
and muted tongue
yearning to find the truth
in living and dying

Innocence

Behold the petal and the leaf
how they hang there forgetful
as a whispered protest
a passionate sin in form
and in shape a complaining deceit
while the earth turns
on its amber curve
tumbling in its relentless drive
toward an unseen millennium
later, to erase the feelings of
uncertainty
we embrace the answer
fair as the lenten lily
which holds within
its fluted innocence
a desire resembling
our common awareness
a thought that ends in misty shock
a breathless glimpse
of time and space imprisoning
reality with a sigh

About the Author

Norine Spurling was born in the semi-tropical islands of Bermuda. As a child she attended painting classes with a local watercolor artist who encouraged her to look at art as a career choice. Her parents sent her to Philadelphia where she studied at Moore College of Art, and later at the Pennsylvania Academy of Fine Art. Two prominent women artists, whose work has been an influence and who studied at these institutions, are Mary Cassatt and Alice Neal.

After having lived in California for several years and raising a family, she moved to Western New York, where she completed her formal education at the State University of New York at Buffalo (UB), and went on to teach drawing there for several years.

While teaching a class in the Black Mountain program at UB she met Jimmie Gilliam, who was teaching a writing class there. At this time she began to reflect on her youthful interest in creative writing and was inspired to enroll in a writing workshop with Jimmie. She then took workshops with other Buffalo poets, like Anne Goldsmith and Jorge Guitart.

Norine is one of the founding members of Women of the Crooked Circle writing group.

www.ingramcontent.com/pod-product-compliance
Lightning Source LLC
Chambersburg PA
CBHW020932090426
42736CB00010B/1117